FAIRACRES PUBLICATIONS 206

STILL LISTENING

Sowing the Seeds of the Jesus Prayer

BRUCE BATSTONE CJN

SLG Press

First Edition 2023

Fairacres Publications No. 206

Print ISBN 978-0-7283-0363-8
Fairacres Publications Series ISSN 0307-1405

Edited and typeset in Palatino Linotype by Julia Craig-McFeely

Biblical quotations are taken from the New Revised Standard Version of the Bible unless otherwise noted

SLG Press
Convent of the Incarnation
Fairacres • Oxford
www.slgpress.co.uk

Printed by
Grosvenor Group Ltd, Loughton, Essex

CONTENTS

for
Trevor Williamson
(1954–2021)

Preface

On a dark winter's night in 2008, a group of us gather in a circle in St Pancras Old Church, a small building on a site of continuous Christian witness since the year 314, tucked just behind St Pancras International Station. As we settle and some instructions are given, I begin to intone quietly the words *Jesus, Son of God, have mercy on me.* I repeat these words over and over again, and after one hundred repetitions I stop speaking and the group continues to pray in a deep silence.

I had first heard of the Jesus Prayer many years before in a book by Br Ramon SSF.[1] This Franciscan hermit wrote very persuasively of the power of this way of prayer, a way that kept reappearing in my reading and in the experience of people I met, and that I have now been practising myself since then. After our session together in St Pancras Old Church all those years ago, I still have conversations with people who were there about how they pray the Jesus Prayer as they walk the city streets, as they travel on buses or on the Tube, as they cycle, or as they sit at home. From these experiences I have come more and more to see the Jesus Prayer as a way of praying well suited to the urban life, a form of attentiveness practice that can help us grow in God-experience amongst the changes and chances of metropolitan living.

I am grateful to those with whom I have spoken about the Jesus Prayer, and whose questions and queries have enhanced my own explorations. I am very grateful to my teachers: Br Ramon SSF; Bishop Simon Barrington-Ward; St Theophan the Recluse, and a whole host of others that I have never met but from whom, through

[1] Brother Ramon SSF, *Praying the Jesus Prayer: A Contemporary Introduction to an Ancient Method of Contemplative Prayer* (Marshall Pickering, 1988).

their writings, I have learned so much. I am grateful to my fellow Companions of Julian, many of whom also pray the Jesus Prayer, who have helped me to see the way it can live within us. Thanks to all who accompany me on my way of faith, all whom I have the privilege to serve as a priest; and those Pastoral Assistants, many now priests themselves, who have helped me to grow and develop, and especially one whose own interest in hesychia was a great inspiration to me. Also, thanks to my colleagues and students of the Ignatian Spirituality Course. It is they, as well as the people of God in the parishes of Old St Pancras, and latterly Hornsey, whose encouragement has helped me to believe in myself as a teacher.

STILL LISTENING

1
Hesychia, the Home of the Jesus Prayer

While staying at Julian House, the monastery of the Order of Julian of Norwich in Wisconsin, as part of a sabbatical in 2010, I was struck by a beautiful icon, painted by one of the nuns, hanging in the guests' sitting room. It is a picture of Jesus teaching Mary of Bethany. She is sitting at His feet, listening with full and rapt attention.

> Now as they went on their way, he entered a certain village, where a woman named Martha welcomed him into her home. She had a sister named Mary, who sat at the Lord's feet and listened to what he was saying. But Martha was distracted by her many tasks; so she came to him and asked, 'Lord, do you not care that my sister has left me to do all the work by myself? Tell her then to help me.' But the Lord answered her, 'Martha, Martha, you are worried and distracted by many things; there is need of only one thing. Mary has chosen the better part, which will not be taken away from her.' (Luke 10:38–42)

I had gone to Julian House Monastery to pray, but as is always the case, I confronted the problem that I know I share with many other Christians: How do we pray? How can we listen attentively to our Lord like Mary of Bethany?

The problem was not external noise and distraction; the horarium of the monastery allows for an atmosphere very conducive to prayer. The challenge was dealing with my internal noise that distracts and seems to prohibit my prayer. When I try to pray, what I am met with in my mind is something similar to a snow scene one finds in seaside souvenirs, a snowglobe. It is very difficult to see what is inside the globe when it is shaken because of all the activity, the bits of 'snow' floating around. Once the movement has settled, there is clarity, stillness. It makes it easier to see, to listen. Clarity makes it easier to pray, but how can I achieve clarity?

The Jesus Prayer, sometimes referred to as the Prayer of the Heart, is partly a way of collecting those thoughts and distractions, a way to recollect oneself and try and stay, even if momentarily, in a repose of stillness; thus, a place where it is possible to begin to listen to God. The prayer encourages a simple sense of presence, a state of 'imageless gazing'.[1] As Christians we wish to be close to God and to be able to trust Him; to cast our anxieties upon Him in patient trust and faith—as a child with its parent. We wish to grow in love of Him, and be filled with His love, to be able to be as close to Him as Jesus was; to be still, at rest in the arms of the God who calls us and loves us, drawing us ever closer to himself, and surrender all we are to Him.

There are many ways described in text and words that seek to help the pilgrim on a journey of prayer to deal with distractions, this internal noise. There is 'Centering Prayer', derived in part from the anonymous English classic *The Cloud of Unknowing*, an anonymous spiritual guide on contemplative prayer written in Middle English in the latter half of the fourteenth century. There is Christian Meditation, a similar approach to prayer advocated by the Benedictine John Main (1926–1982) and continued by the World Community for Christian Meditation. There are ways of praying with the breath, and ways to practise attentiveness that are shared with other faith traditions. More recently the practice of 'Mindfulness' has become widespread and is used in

[1] Kallistos Ware, 'How Do We Enter the Heart', in Bernadette Dieker and Jonthan Montaldo, eds., *Merton and Hesychasm* (Fons Vitae, 2003), 14.

many walks of life, both secular and sacred. These are all ways to practise what we call recollection, and among them is the way of hesychia, which I have personally found the most rich and helpful. Hesychia is a Greek word (ησυχία), meaning *rest, quiet* or *tranquillity* and the word is used to describe the mystical theology of the Jesus Prayer. It grew out of Eastern Christianity: our teachers are the Desert Fathers and Mothers from the fourth century, and much of their teaching on hesychia and the Jesus Prayer is found in *The Philokalia.*

The Philokalia is a collection of spiritual writings by Greek monastic authors covering a period of about 1000 years. It was compiled by St Nikodemos of the Holy Mountain and St Makarios of Corinth, and was published in Venice in 1782. Martin Laird, a writer whose work on this subject has helped my understanding of the practice of the Jesus Prayer a great deal, uses an example from the author J. D. Salinger to explain with beautiful simplicity what this collection of wisdom is. In Salinger's narrative Franny Glass discovers the world of the Jesus Prayer in the midst of a crisis in her life and tries to explain to her inattentive and self-absorbed boyfriend how she has started to pray it after reading *The Way of the Pilgrim*:

> '… the pilgrim—this simple peasant—started the whole pilgrimage to find out what it means in the Bible when it says you're supposed to pray without ceasing. And then he meets this *starets*—this very advanced religious person I mentioned, the one who'd been studying the "Philokalia" for years and years and years.' Franny stopped suddenly to reflect, to organize. 'Well, the *starets* tells him about the Jesus Prayer first of all. "Lord Jesus Christ, have mercy on me." I mean that's what it is. And he explains to him that those are the best words to use when you pray. Especially the word "mercy," because it's such a really enormous word and can mean so many things. I mean it doesn't just have to mean *mercy*.'[2]

[2] J. D. Salinger, *Franny and Zoey* (Baker Books, 1961), 36.

As time has passed, certain techniques and forms of words have come to represent the Jesus Prayer. Most commonly the form of words has evolved into *Jesus Christ, Son of God, have mercy on me* or *Jesus Christ, Son of God, have mercy on me, a sinner.* As well as being about prayer, it is important for us to understand that the Jesus Prayer is about a way of life, a hesychastic way of attentiveness to the name of Christ and his presence; a way that may lead to dwelling in the glory of God.

The road to our pearl of great price, to sit with Mary at the feet of Jesus, is filled with obstacles; this is problematic when deep prayer requires us to seek a profound inner stillness. Like tuning in a radio, we want to get beyond the crackles and the fuzziness that so often fills our minds. We want to come to a clarity, a rest, a stillness. It has commonly been the practice of Christians to seek this quiet and stillness by retreating to a place of peace and focus. This flight into solitude creates an atmosphere conducive to the prayer we seek. Hesychastic life is an attempt to find that stillness and peace within ourselves; to move apart from the distractions of the mind, to turn into the peace of solitude within ourselves, even though physically we have not moved anywhere. The hesychast is one who listens, who lets the prayer speak; the one who is silent, allowing God to speak.[3]

We might describe this whole area of the study of prayer of the heart as *recollection*: re-collecting ourselves, bringing ourselves back to our home, to God. A writer I have only recently discovered, a man firmly rooted in the Western tradition and one who had a great influence upon Teresa of Avila and St John of the Cross, is the Franciscan friar and writer Francisco de Osuna. He lived from 1492 to 1540, born in the Seville region of Spain on the eve of that country's golden age of mysticism characterized particularly by the leaders of the Carmelite reform. In the midst

[3] See Kallistos Ware, 'Silence in Prayer: The Meaning of Hesychia', in Jonathan Montaldo, ed., *Merton and Hesychasm* (Fons Vitae, 2003), 14.

of the controversy over the nature of true interior prayer that raged during the 1520s, Osuna wrote some practical guidelines, maxims if you will, arranged into Spiritual Alphabets. The best known perhaps is his *Third Spiritual Alphabet*:

> The recollected person should be like the ark of God, which never left the temple's most interior and secret chapel, a place of refuge few entered. When the ark was carried through the desert they enveloped it in three coverings so it would be well recollected and safely enclosed ... A secret, recollected place is necessary to invite you to enter within yourself. For the wise man says: "Entering my house, I shall rest here, for her conversation is not bitter, nor her company tedious, but full of joy and gladness." If you enter your house willingly and are desirous to see your cell and go immediately to it, feeling that one hour away from it is like a day, and a day is like a year, and if you return with great desire, you will be totally content in your house—that is, in both body and soul—for their conversation will not taste bitter, unless you bring bitterness in, and their company will neither anger, nor aggrieve nor disagree with you. On the contrary, your body will be pleased and your soul will rejoice because of the heavenly visit that occurs more often when we are drawn into rather than out of ourselves.[4]

It is from this place of recollection that the best-discerned actions and judgements are made. It is the place where I have set aside my ego. Trying to follow the road without being diverted by each thought and reaction, each spark that sets fire to our anger, our resentment, our jealousy. It is trying to be vigilant and not begin a conversation with the thoughts. This requires awareness, watchfulness, and attention.

St John Cassian (360–435 AD), travelled widely in the monastic circles of his day. During his travels he received teaching first-hand from the great fathers and mothers of monasticism of

[4] Francisco de Osuna OFM, *The Third Spiritual Alphabet*, trans. Mary E. Giles, Preface by Kieran Kavanaugh OCD (Paulist Press, 1981), 253.

Egypt and Syria. His best-known works, *The Institutes* and *The Conferences* bring together the wisdom of the Desert Fathers and Mothers with the monastic traditions of the East and the West.[5] The first conference 'The Goal and Objective of the Monk', describes the thoughts that enter the mind as coming from three sources: the devil, ourselves, and God. He says that our minds are working constantly, and it is our choice to which thoughts we attach ourselves:

> The activity of the heart is compared, not inappropriately, to that of a mill which is activated by the circular motion of water. The mill cannot cease operations at all so long as it is driven round by the pressure of water and it, then, becomes quite feasible for the person in charge to decide whether he prefers wheat or barley or darnel to be ground. And one thing is clear. Only that will be ground which is fed in by the one who is in charge.[6]

Cassian goes on to warn the reader of the consequences if the monk does not make every effort to keep his mind recollected in this way of considering the thoughts and behaviours to which he allows himself to become attached, and the dangers to the monk's search for closeness to God:

> ... if we are overcome by sloth or carelessness, if we give ourselves over to dangerous and useless chattering, if we are caught up in worldly cares and profitless worries, there will follow in effect from this a harvest of tares to serve as a ministry of death to our hearts. As the Lord our Saviour proclaimed, where treasure lies for our works and our hopes, our hearts will of necessity abide there too.[7]

---

[5] John Cassian, *The Conferences*, trans. Colm Luibheid, Classics of Western Spirituality (Paulist Press, 1985); John Cassian, *The Institutes*, trans. Boniface Ramsey OP (Paulist Press, 2000).

[6] John Cassian, *The Conferences*, 52.

[7] Ibid.

The recollection being described is called 'watchfulness' in this particular part of the tradition, and this watchfulness is a grace gifted to us from a place of stillness. Like a sentry, the heart is guarded by this watchfulness so that the direction can be carefully held. Sometimes we can feel dispersed, 'all over the place'. We want to bring all the parts together, to settle them in their rightful place, like the particles settling in the snowglobe. The Jesus Prayer is about re-integration, bringing back together, creating some order and rest. This vigilant watchfulness is often described in the writings on hesychia as a form of spiritual warfare, a battle between thoughts that help and encourage, and thoughts that take us away from God:

> If you wish to engage in spiritual warfare, let that little animal, the spider, always be your example for stillness of the heart; otherwise you will not be as still in your intellect as you should be. The spider hunts small flies: but you will continually slay 'the children of Babylon' (Ps 137:9) if during your struggle you are as still as the spider.[8]

Most of us who try to practise the Jesus Prayer are neither monks nor nuns. We just want to pray better. What I think the wisdom of *The Philokalia* tells us is that prayer is something to work at, it is a discipline that we try to inhabit; a way of living and praying which, though it will take time, will in the long run form us into people able to listen to the words of Jesus with less distraction, to be more attentive, even as Mary of Bethany.

[8] 'Hesychyos', in G. E. H. Palmer, Kallistos Ware, Philip Sherrard, trans., *The Philokalia: The Complete Text*, Vol. 1 (Faber & Faber, 2011), 229.

2
A Gutsy Prayer

We can see that our task, if we wish to emulate the attentiveness of Mary, rather than to continue to live the more dispersed existence of her sister Martha, is to live a recollected life. The writings on hesychia found in *The Philokalia,* talk about the Jesus Prayer, a form of words to which we can attend, and which can help to enable more recollection within ourselves. To continue the image from Cassian introduced above, praying this way can help us to ensure that only the most wholesome grains take up the energy of the mill. These wholesome grains are the words of the Jesus Prayer. With their help we can concentrate and unify an ever-active mind by feeding it with a single thought, by nourishing it on a spiritual diet 'that is at once rich yet exceedingly simple'.[9]

The words of the Jesus Prayer can vary. The forms most commonly used are *Jesus Christ, Son of God, have mercy on me, a sinner;* and *Jesus, Son of God, have mercy*. These simple words contain the central message of the gospel. They are the call of Bartimaeus, who recognizes Jesus for who he is:

> They came to Jericho. As he and his disciples and a large crowd were leaving Jericho, Bartimaeus son of Timaeus, a blind beggar, was sitting by the roadside. When he heard that it was Jesus of Nazareth, he began to shout out and say, "Jesus, Son of David, have mercy on me!" Many sternly ordered him to be quiet, but he cried out even more loudly, "Son of David, have mercy on me!" (Mark 10:46–8)

---

[9] Ware, 'Silence in Prayer', 27.

It is also the prayer of the tax collector, who knows his need for God's love and forgiveness:

> But the tax collector, standing far off, would not even look up to heaven, but was beating his breast and saying, "God, be merciful to me, a sinner!" (Luke 18:13).

In *The Pilgrim's Tale*, also known as *The Way of the Pilgrim*, the author recounts the teaching of a monk of Athos who 'prayed without ceasing and was experienced in the interior prayer of the heart':

> Even its very form shows the greatness of the Jesus Prayer ... for it consists in two parts. In the first of them, that is, *Lord Jesus Christ, Son of God*, it introduces the mind to the history of the life of Jesus Christ or, as the holy fathers put it, 'it abbreviates in itself the holy gospel'. In the second part, that is, *have mercy on me, a sinner*, it presents the history of our weakness and sinfulness. It is remarkable that the desire and petition of a poor, sinful, and humble soul cannot be expressed more wisely, more basically, and more distinctly than with these words, 'have mercy on me!'[10]

Some practitioners shorten the prayer to *Jesus, have mercy*. Some, although more rarely, shorten it simply to *Jesus*. On a visit to Mount Athos, a wellspring of the ancient hesychastic tradition, I was lucky enough to receive teaching from one of the monks who suggested I use the simpler form, *Lord Jesus Christ, have mercy on me*. If the Jesus Prayer is to be of the tradition of hesychia, the name of Jesus must be part of it. It is this fact that accounts for the uniqueness of the Jesus Prayer within the spiritual traditions of recollection. It is a confession of faith, and not just an incantation to relax us. In using the name of Jesus, we are invoking the Holy Name which has within it a sacramental value. It is in using the name that we render present the One

---

[10] Aleksei Pentkovsky, ed., T. Allan Smith, trans., *The Pilgrim's Tale*, Classics of Western Spirituality (Paulist Press, 1999), 161–2.

whose name is being spoken, suggesting a grace-giving connection between Jesus and the Name. This is part of a long biblical tradition: Kallistos Ware, one of the greatest contemporary writers on the Jesus Prayer, explains,

> God's name is intimately linked with His person, and so the invocation of the divine name possesses a sacramental character, serving as an efficacious sign of His invisible presence and action.[11]

To appreciate the uniqueness of the Jesus Prayer as the Prayer of the Name, we need to reflect also on the world from which this prayer has come to us. In understanding this, we can understand better the precious jewel that we have in our hands. The Jesus Prayer occupies a specific place within the spiritual tradition and is a central pillar of the Orthodox tradition of Christianity. Kallistos Ware writes that the Jesus Prayer,

> has become for innumerable Eastern Christians over the centuries the standard path, the royal highway. And not for Eastern Christians only: in the meeting between Orthodoxy and the West over the past seventy years, probably no element in the Orthodox heritage has aroused such intense interest as the Jesus Prayer.[12]

First, we need to see the deep connection articulated here between what it means to be a person and what is means to be one who prays, and how our personhood can be re-integrated through our prayer.

> The human is built in such a way as to commune with God in the silent depths of a heart enlightened by the grace of baptism. But, because of the weakness of our nature, such communion seems distant and practically impossible. Part of the problem is

[11] Kallistos Ware, *The Power of the Name: The Jesus Prayer in Orthodox Spirituality*, Fairacres Publications 43 (SLG Press, 1987, 3rd edition 2022), 16.

[12] Idem, 5.

the obsessive tendencies or patterns of the mind called "the passions". These passions are stirred up by afflictive thoughts with the result that "bit by bit, one drifts away from what one is supposed to be doing [praying] into a world of fantasy". Growing gradually out of touch with reality, the Christian thus grows out of touch with God. The journey of prayer is the working out of the grace of baptism, which becomes in a practical way a battle against the inner noise and chaos of endless thoughts and mental chatter that keep our attention riveted to the surface of life and therefore ignorant of the silent depths within, where God dwells. As a remedy to this struggle of the human condition, the *Philokalia* advises stillness, watchfulness and the Jesus Prayer.[13]

God dwells within the human person: this is the gift of grace given at baptism.

> True prayer, then, signifies the rediscovery and 'manifestation' of baptismal grace. To pray is to pass from the state where grace is present in our hearts secretly and unconsciously, to the point of full inner perception and conscious awareness when we experience and feel the activity of the spirit directly and immediately.[14]

Ware goes on to explain that the writers at the time of *The Philokalia* had no concept of things physiological, such as blood circulation, that we are aware of now. They simply knew that if the heart stopped beating then you died; so the heart was viewed very much as the meeting place between the Divine and the human, between the spiritual and the physical. Thus, prayer came to be defined in three main ways: the first is oral prayer, prayer with the lips. The second is what we might call prayer of the *guts*: prayer using not the intellect, the faculties to think and

[13] Martin Laird, '"Continually Breathe Jesus Christ": Stillness and Watchfulness in the *Philokalia*', *Communio* 34 (2007), 245.

[14] Ware, *The Power of the Name*, 3.

to consider, but the place of inner vision that is able to comprehend spiritual truths, not with reasoned arguments but more directly. This is prayer located in the realm commonly described as the 'guts', that place of discerning intuitive wisdom. The third phase is the prayer of the heart, the form of prayer whereby the intellect is brought down into the realm of the heart, where the reasoning mind and the 'gutsy' discernment meet. So the heart becomes seen as the centre of the person, the place of meeting of the person with God. Thus the prayer of the heart,

> is the total person, body, soul and spirit. But since the heart is the place of divine indwelling, prayer of the heart is prayer in which it is not only I who speak, but it is the prayer which Christ and the Holy Spirit are saying in me.[15]

In this prayer, we enter our very selves and discover the dimensions of our personhood. Once we begin to feel more integrated, we can try and place all that we are under God who dwells at our centre. It means to bring together all aspects of our personhood, to reunite the parts of our identifiable 'self'. So, prayer is about healing: *Lord Have Mercy*. It is about repentance, central to our lives as Christians and particularly voiced and valued in the Orthodox tradition. It is that sense of being brought back to our rightful place in relationship with God, that part of us that is like the Prodigal Son returning home once again to be one with God.

---

[15] Cf. Ware, 'How Do We Enter the Heart', 9.

3
The Practice

How do we say the Jesus Prayer? It could be said that instructions fall into two parts, reflecting two ways in which the prayer can be used. Either it is used as an intentional practice that is prayed at specific times and perhaps as part of a regular prayer time, sometimes called the 'fixed' way. The alternative, which might be described as a more free or informal practice, is praying the Jesus Prayer randomly, at different times of the day, when we are involved in different activities or moved spontaneously to prayer, sometimes called the 'free' way.

I mainly immerse myself in the tradition of the Jesus Prayer intentionally, within a dedicated prayer time, and the teachings I have followed about this way suggest to begin by saying the words of the prayer out loud, slowly repeating them in turn over and over again. As time passes, it may be that the repetition becomes more internal, repeating the prayer under the breath for a time, and eventually silently, listening to the words within oneself as one might listen to the waves breaking on the shore. The purpose of this form of prayer is to focus attention on words, and using that focus to regain attention when this has been lost in the inevitable distractions that fill our minds. For many people, a secondary support to their prayer focus is the engagement of the sense of touch, joining the actions of the body to the mind. This helps me too, and when I pray in this way I tend to use a rosary or prayer rope. The words can vary, as I have said; my preference for many years was to say *Jesus Christ, Son of God, have mercy on me*, and it is this form of words I will use for the sake of teaching about the practice here. Building on the engagement of the body, I find it is best to sit or kneel in a place where you are comfortable and can relax. Focus your attention on your breathing, and as you breathe in say the words, "Jesus Christ, Son of God", and as you breathe out "have mercy on me". Do this gently and you will find that your breathing will slow. If you use a rope, touch a knot as you say each prayer. If distracting thoughts intrude, try to detach from them by attaching yourself to the words of the prayer. They may be thoughts of resentment, anger or anxiety; they may be practical thoughts like a shopping list. It is hard to avoid these distracting thoughts, but try not to be captivated by them, or anxious about their intrusion; just focus on the words and the rope. These words are more than a mantra, they are an evocation of the Name of Jesus and He is present with us as we pray.

The more spontaneous, or 'free' way of praying, is described in *The Way of the Pilgrim*. This popular anonymous work brought the Jesus Prayer to the West. It is a highly attractive little book, translated from the Russian and dating from the nineteenth century, and has been one of the main sources for the interest in the Jesus Prayer in the West. In it the pilgrim of the title prays the Jesus Prayer as he walks. Indeed, he continues the prayer whilst engaged in other activities too, as is also the case for many of the other characters that he meets whose conversations and tales make the story so accessible and enjoyable. The prayer is said whilst they are engaged in the normal practices of the day, and this is something that I find very helpful too. It can be recited during those scattered moments that may otherwise be lost to prayer as I garden or sweep the floor; as I walk to the Tube station, or stand waiting for the bus; as I sit or stand wedged into a stressful packed train carriage, or walk through the busy streets around my home. I may say it at times when I am engaged in routine or semi-automatic activities such as dressing or washing up. The Jesus Prayer is never out of place, and always acts as a way of gathering my consciousness from a place of fragmentation towards a wholeness in God, rather than being someone tossed around by my response to whatever is happening to me at the time. Indeed, this is central to the theology of the Jesus Prayer tradition, that our personhood only has true meaning in Christ, and the Jesus Prayer draws us to this deeper place of identity.

4
Some Questions and Queries

How many times should I say the prayer?

There can be some confusion about this; the answer can vary according to your circumstances. *The Way of the Pilgrim* has been partly responsible for some of this confusion. In the book, the pilgrim is asked by his spiritual director to say the prayer six thousand times in a day. I am reliably informed by many whose specialist knowledge on this subject is far deeper and wider than my own, that such an instruction is very unusual and may well have been a test of the obedience to the prayer of that particular pilgrim rather than a literal target for everyone. The number of times does not matter, and the rosary or prayer rope containing 30, 50 or perhaps 100 knots is there to assist our attention rather than to keep count.

How fast should I be saying the prayer?

This will vary depending on circumstances and need. I find that praying one hundred knots can take me half an hour or longer if I am saying the prayer slowly and leaving a gap between each of the words. At other times this number of prayers can take as little as fifteen minutes if my body has not relaxed as much as I would wish. Again, I would caution against being too concerned about these things. Most important is that we pray the prayer as attentively as we can at the time we are praying it, really seeking to focus upon the Name of Christ and His presence with us. As St Theophan the Recluse says,

> Let this be your sole concern, that it [the prayer] should spring up in your heart with quickening power like a fountain of living water. Expel entirely from your mind all thoughts of quantity.[16]

What about use of the breath?

The use of the breath is sometimes considered controversial with the Jesus Prayer. I think it is best to allow the prayer to find your breathing, so ensure that you are breathing in a natural and healthy way, and not changing your breathing to fit the prayer. Some people try to connect the saying of the Jesus Prayer with their heartbeat. This is movingly described in *The Way of the Pilgrim*:

> Form an image of your heart … direct your eyes towards it as though you were looking at it. Listen attentively with your mind to its beating and how it pounds, one beat after another. The holy fathers call this 'bringing the mind out of one's head into one's heart'. When you have mastered this, begin to fit the words of the prayer to every beat of the heart, all the while looking at it. Thus, with the first beat, say or think 'Lord'; with the second, 'Jesus'; with the third, 'Christ'; with the fourth, 'have mercy'; and with the fifth, 'on me'. Repeat this over and over again … Then, once you are used to this, begin to bring the whole Jesus Prayer in and out of your heart in harmony with your breathing, as the fathers teach. That is, as you inhale, say or imagine 'Lord Jesus Christ', and as you exhale, 'have mercy on me'. Devote yourself to this often and as much as you can and you will quickly feel a very pleasant pain in your heart; the warmth and ardour will come.[17]

---

[16] Quoted in Ware, *The Power of the Name*, 11.

[17] Pentkovsky, ed., *The Pilgrim's Tale*, 126.

I have attempted this 'heart-listening' and found that sometimes it has helped and other times it has not, and has just become a distraction. One benefit of trying to connect the prayer to the heartbeat it that it has a rhythmic quality that can complement the prayer well, similar to praying the Jesus Prayer while walking. This guidance is connected to the hesychastic practical teaching which says that, when we pray the Jesus Prayer, we should try to locate the place of the heart and dwell there. In terms that might be in reach of the beginner, my experience is to begin by trying to sit in a place where there are no obvious distractions. Either close your eyes, or look at one point on the floor. As you begin to practise, it may well be that your concentration is in the realm of your head. Try to move the place of focus down to your chest, as though you are leaving the realm of the mind and its thoughts and entering a world much more of experience and feeling. Try to do this each time that you pray and you may well find that you practise yourself into this concept of taking the mind into the heart, a concept that is very difficult to explain in words.

> To accomplish the journey inwards and to attain true prayer, it is required of us to enter into this 'absolute centre', that is, to descend from the intellect into the heart. More exactly, we are called to descend not from but with the intellect. The aim is not just 'prayer of the heart' but 'prayer of the intellect in the heart', for our varied forms of understanding, including our reason, are a gift from God and are to be used in his service, not rejected. This 'union of the intellect with the heart' signifies the reintegration of our fallen and fragmented nature, our restoration to original wholeness.[18]

[18] Ware, *The Power of the Name*, 26.

What are the effects of the Jesus Prayer?

A concept called 'theosis' is central to the Orthodox understanding of prayer. As we pray, God is able to transform us more into his likeness. This growth in love for God is a participation in perichoresis: that is, the dance of life amongst the three persons of the Trinity: Father, Son and Holy Spirit. In the hesychast tradition, this mystery of theosis has often been understood in terms of light, that light of the uncreated Godhead that is neither real nor symbolic. That light such as the transforming light of Mount Tabor that transfigures all of creation. Praying the Jesus Prayer can help us to see the creation more bathed in this light of God:

> When I prayed with my heart, everything around me seemed delightful and marvellous. The trees, the grass, the birds, the air, the light seemed to be telling me that they existed for man's sake, that they witnessed to the love of God for man, that everything proved the love of God for man, that all things prayed to God and sang his praise. Thus it was that I came to understand what *The Philokalia* calls 'the knowledge of the speech of all creatures' … I felt a burning love for Jesus and for all God's creatures.[19]

The prayer creates a sense in the Pilgrim of a oneness with all creation around him. He also reports a sense of lightness and renewed love for the people around him:

> Again I started off on my wanderings. But now I did not walk along as before, filled with care. The invocation of the Name of Jesus gladdened my way. Everybody was kind to me, it was as though everyone loved me. … If anyone harms me I have only to think, 'How sweet is the Prayer of Jesus!' and the injury and the anger alike pass away and I forget it all.[20]

---

[19] *The Pilgrim's Tale,* quoted in Ware, *The Power of the Name,* 38–9.

[20] Quoted in Ware, *The Power of the Name,* 39.

For my own part, I have found that praying the Jesus Prayer has encouraged me to try and stay in the present moment, fixed to the 'now', and the prayer gives a means of excavating the present moment, of helping me to remain in place and think back less. Often in conversations we are thinking about what has just happened, or what is about to happen, and so we find it hard to be present. Common distractions might be associated with fear, or with anger. This I call 'embroidering of the story'. When I try to pray with the Jesus Prayer each morning, I find the distraction is the day that is coming. How will it feel to see that person? Will I be able to speak well into this or that situation? So stories get embroidered around the central factors which are often fear, or anger. How can we stop the embroidery? By sitting with the feeling, to abide in the reality of our bodies; to rest there, and when we get distracted into the past, or into the future, to come back to that point which is about the moment in all its power of rest. This is the moment in which God rests with us, the moment at which Christ embraces and cherishes us:

> To have your attention in the [moment] is not a denial of what is needed in your life. It is recognising what is primary. Then you can deal with what is secondary with great ease. It is not saying "I am not dealing with things any more because there is only the [moment]." No. Find what is primary first, and make the [moment] into your friend, not your enemy. Acknowledge it, honour it. When the [moment] is the foundation and primary focus of your life, then your life unfolds with ease.[21]

I find that to ground myself in the moment with the aid of the prayer calms me, helps me to take each moment as it comes, helps me to know that the Name of Christ I invoke, the presence of Christ with me now, will still be with me in all the 'nows' to

---

[21] Eckhart Tolle, *The Power of Now: A Guide to Spiritual Enlightenment* (Yellow Kite, 2001), 41.

come. I do want to assure the reader that I am nowhere near perfect, but I have experienced that this prayer is like playing an instrument. The more you practise it the better you get; and the more you practise, the more practise you need. And most importantly, the practice of the prayer is about making us available to God in the present moment. It is His grace only that grants the prayer.

This attention to each moment is becoming a common practice for those who care for people struggling with poor mental and physical health. To use exercises with breathing, attending to the here and now, can help people to manage physical and mental pain or anxiety more easily by not allowing themselves to become attached to a train of thought that can bring them into places within themselves that are dark and painful. I want to encourage this, but to remind the reader that such meditation practices, including that of Mindfulness, were not invented in the 1960s or just recently! The tradition of the Jesus Prayer dates from the early centuries of the Christian era; not only does hesychia teach a practice that is beneficial, it also teaches that we believe that we reside in the beauty of the present moment with our Lord Jesus Christ upon whose Divine Name we call, and who promises to be present with us always.

Can we pray the Jesus Prayer together?

Definitely 'yes', particularly in the early stages of practice. Indeed, there is some precedent for this, including a very good book co-written by Br Ramon SSF and Bp Simon Barrington-Ward called *Praying the Jesus Prayer Together.* For a week they prayed for an hour together, 200 knots aloud then a period of silence, and this speaking out loud is perhaps the best way to pray the prayer with others. In a group, I will often say the words of the prayer for a time and then we go into silence. This allows for us each to pray at our own pace and avoid distracting others. In terms of ongoing practice, the prayer is about our own journey into God, and therefore most developed practice is going to take place alone.

Throughout *The Philokalia*, the reader is told that anyone practising the Jesus Prayer needs the guidance of a spiritual director. This may, of course, be true. Anyone seeking to grow in their prayer needs guidance and the encouraging accountability that a spiritual director or soul-friend can bring. There is, however, a lack of directors experienced in the practice of the Jesus Prayer, so I would tend to encourage anyone who feels drawn to the Jesus Prayer simply to begin. In the early stages good teaching and support can be drawn from published literature and well-sourced online materials. I would also encourage that those who use the prayer might want to try and pray together with others sometimes, to support each another, and thereby begin to widen that support to others. This will be beneficial in the absence of any specialist help, but also complements it.

What about intercessory prayer?

Kallistos Ware tells us that praying the Jesus Prayer as an aid to intercession is not part of the hesychast tradition:

> Can the Jesus Prayer be used as a form of intercession? The reply must be that, in the strict sense, it is distinct from intercessory prayer. As an expression of non-discursive, non-iconic 'waiting upon God', it does not involve the explicit recalling and mention of particular names. We simply turn to Jesus. It is true, of course, that in turning to Jesus we do not thereby turn away from our fellow humans. All those whom we love are already embraced in his heart, loved by him infinitely more than by us, and so in the end through the Jesus Prayer we find them again in him; invoking the name, we enter more and more fully into Christ's overflowing love for the entire world. But if we are following

the Hesychast pattern of the Jesus Prayer, we do not bring others before him specifically by name, or hold them deliberately in our mind, as we recite the Invocation.[22]

Some writers, such as Br Ramon SSF and Bp Simon Barrington-Ward, do write about the Jesus Prayer as a form of intercessory prayer, but this is a digression from hesychastic teaching in its strict sense.

Is the intentional or formal way of praying the Jesus Prayer really necessary when the spontaneous way seems more natural and accessible?

The informal way of reciting the words of the Jesus Prayer more spontaneously might be compared to practising the Presence of God. The book, *The Practice of the Presence of God,* is a collection of writings originating from seventeenth-century France, by a Carmelite friar called Brother Lawrence of the Resurrection.[23] The little book encourages us to follow the example of the prayer of the author who was able to find God in the pots and pans of the kitchen, and be ever mindful of God, keeping attention upon Him in all the activities of the day. The similarity lies only in the fact that Br Lawrence cautions those benefitting from his counsel that such prayer amidst activity is nourished by the formal prayer times of the monastery. He assumes that the prayer practices that help us to be detached from distractions are also practised within a more formal prayer time, which holds the one who is praying in the way that riverbanks hold the flow of water. His way of praying, therefore, is not just a prayer amidst action,

[22] Ware, *The Power of the Name,* 41.

[23] First published in 1692, there have been many editions and translations. One respected edition that is as true as possible to the original is: Brother Lawrence of the Resurrection OCD, *The Practice of the Presence of God,* trans. E. M. Blaiklock, Hodder Christian Classics (Hodder & Stoughton, 1997).

it is a way to pray through all the informal and formal spaces of the day; a way of prayer that is about attention upon God; a journey of prayer that is only possible through the attentiveness developed in the more prolonged prayer typical of the Carmelite charism. This is well known through the works of St John of the Cross and St Teresa of Avila. I suppose what this tells us is that, at its best, the free and fixed forms of the prayer nourish each other, and help to build a holistic practice of prayer enfolding all areas of our lives.

5
Concluding Thoughts

When we pray, our intention is to entwine our lives with God, who has entwined himself with us to the depth of our very being through His love shown to us in Christ. We seek to become closer and closer to Him, that our humanity may come to its home, which is God's Divinity. This requires that we allow the Spirit to work in us, to help us set aside layer upon layer of selfishness and self-absorption, to let go of what we call our ego, to become entirely the fire of Divine Life. As St John tells us:

> Now by this we may be sure that we know him, if we obey his commandments. Whoever says, "I have come to know him," but does not keep his commandments, is a liar, and in such a person the truth does not exist; but whoever obeys his word, truly in this person the love of God has reached perfection. By this we may be sure that we are in him: whoever says, "I abide in him," ought to walk just as he walked. (1 John 2:3–6)

This growth in prayer for which many strive, a prayer that we hope forms us more into God's intention for us, is a long and hard path; the greatest guides in prayer warn us to expect difficulties and encourage us to seek guidance and to follow a well-trodden path. This path, a discipline of some sort of regular immersion into the silence of contemplative prayer, has been for many the way of the heart in the Jesus Prayer. When we pray the Jesus Prayer we are immersing ourselves in a tradition of prayer that is very ancient, a tradition from which we can receive much and, by participating, to which we can also contribute.

It is firmly in the contemplative mould, a way of practising the prayer of the heart that can be easily adapted to a contemporary lifestyle. As I described in the Preface, its flexibility and adaptability means it can be easily translated to our modern lives. Especially, it can help us grow in attentiveness in our increasingly urban existence.

Praying the Jesus Prayer encourages us to a disciplined life of attention to God. Increasingly, individuals and Christian churches are seeking help in developing rhythms, or rules, of life that help them to form a life of discipleship and faith. The tradition of hesychia, within which there is a long-held custom of spiritual accompaniment or direction, can help our journey towards a more integrated practice of our faithfulness to Christ.

Our world grows smaller each day as, through technology and experience, we learn more and more about the lives of our brothers and sisters across the globe. The Jesus Prayer is an ecumenical prayer; hesychia is a gift to us from the East, a way of understanding our prayer that is perfectly adaptable to our own Western Christian culture and modern way of life.

Bibliography

Simon Barrington-Ward, *The Jesus Prayer: A Way to Contemplation* (Pauline Books & Media, 2011).

John Cassian, *The Conferences*, trans. Colm Luibheid, Classics of Western Spirituality (Paulist Press, 1985).

——, *The Institutes*, trans. Boniface Ramsey OP (Paulist Press, 2000).

James S. Cutsinger, ed., *Paths to the Heart: Sufism and the Christian East*, Perennial Philosophy Series (World Wisdom Books, 2002).

Bernadette Dieker and Jonathan Montaldo, eds., *Merton & Hesychasm: The Prayer of the Heart; the Eastern Church* (Fons Vitae, 2003).

Martin Laird, '"Continually Breathe Jesus Christ": Stillness and Watchfulness in the *Philokalia*', *Communio* 34 (2007).

Brother Lawrence of the Resurrection OCD, *The Practice of the Presence of God*, trans. E. M. Blaiklock, Hodder Christian Classics (Hodder & Stoughton, 1997).

'A Monk of the Eastern Church' [Archimandrite Lev Gillet], *The Jesus Prayer: Introduction to Orthodox Spirituality* (St Vladimir's Seminary Press, 1987).

Francisco de Osuna OFM, *The Third Spiritual Alphabet*, trans. Mary E. Giles, Preface by Kieran Kavanaugh OCD (Paulist Press, 1981).

G. E. H. Palmer, Kallistos Ware, Philip Sherrard, trans., *The Philokalia: The Complete Text*, Vol. 1 (Faber & Faber, 2011).

Aleksei Pentkovsky, ed. and introd., T. Allan Smith, trans., *The Pilgrim's Tale*, Classics of Western Spirituality (Paulist Press, 1999).

Brother Ramon SSF, *Praying the Jesus Prayer: A Contemporary Introduction to an Ancient Method of Contemplative Prayer* (Marshall Pickering, 1988).

Brother Ramon SSF, *The Heart of Prayer: Finding a Time, a Place and a Way to Pray* (Marshall Pickering, 1995).

Brother Ramon SSF, Simon Barrington-Ward, Frederica Mathewes-Green, *Praying the Jesus Prayer Together* (Hendrickson Publishers, 2004).

Eckhart Tolle, *The Power of Now: A Guide to Spiritual Enlightenment* (Yellow Kite, 2001).

Metropolitan Kallistos Ware, 'How Do We Enter the Heart, and What Do We Find When We Enter?', in Dieker and Montaldo, eds., *Merton and Hesychasm*, 3–16.

——, *The Power of the Name: The Jesus Prayer in Orthodox Spirituality*, Fairacres Publications 43 (SLG Press, 1997; 3rd edn 2022).

——, 'Silence in Prayer: The Meaning of Hesychia', in Dieker and Montaldo, eds., *Merton and Hesychasm*, 17–40.

There are many editions of *The Cloud of Unknowing*; I have suggested one 'classic' and two good modern editions. There are also numerous free editions available online.

Dennis J. Billy, ed., *The Cloud of Unknowing* (Liguori Publications, 2014).

Carmen Acevedo Butcher, ed., *The Cloud of Unknowing* (Shambhala Pocket Edition, 2018).

James Walsh, ed., *The Cloud of Unknowing* (Paulist Press, 1981).

SLG Press books about the Jesus Prayer

Andy Lord, *River of the Spirit: The Spirituality of Simon Barrington-Ward*, Fairacres Publications 189 (SLG Press, 2021).

Sr Pauline Margaret CHN, *The Jesus Prayer: Gospel Soundings*, Fairacres Publications 154 (SLG Press, 2008).

James F. Wellington, *Journeying with the Jesus Prayer*, Fairacres Publications 186 (SLG Press, 2020).

Metropolitan Kallistos Ware, *The Power of the Name: The Jesus Prayer in Orthodox Spirituality*, Fairacres Publications 43 (SLG Press, 1997; 3rd edn 2022).

Chotki Prayer Ropes

33, 50 or 100 knots

available from www.slgpress.co.uk

SLG PRESS PUBLICATIONS

FP1 *Prayer and the Life of Reconciliation* Gilbert Shaw (1969)
FP2 *Aloneness Not Loneliness* Mother Mary Clare SLG (1969)
FP4 *Intercession* Mother Mary Clare SLG (1969)
FP8 *Prayer: Extracts from the Teaching of Fr Gilbert Shaw* Gilbert Shaw (1973)
FP12 *Learning to Pray* Mother Mary Clare SLG (1970)
FP15 *Death, the Gateway to Life* Gilbert Shaw (1971)
FP16 *The Victory of the Cross* Dumitru Stăniloae (1970, 3rd edn 2023)
FP26 *The Message of Saint Seraphim* Irina Gorainov (1974)
FP28 *Julian of Norwich: Four Studies to Commemorate the Sixth Centenary of the Revelations of Divine Love* Sister Benedicta Ward SLG, Sister Eileen Mary SLG ed. A. M. Allchin (1973)
FP43 *The Power of the Name: The Jesus Prayer in Orthodox Spirituality* Kallistos Ware (1974)
FP46 *Prayer and Contemplation* and *Distractions are for Healing* Robert Llewelyn (1975)
FP48 *The Wisdom of the Desert Fathers* trans. Sister Benedicta Ward SLG (1975)
FP50 *Letters of Saint Antony the Great* trans. Derwas Chitty (1975, 2nd edn 2021)
FP54 *From Loneliness to Solitude* Roland Walls (1976)
FP55 *Theology and Spirituality* Andrew Louth (1976, rev. 1978)
FP61 *Kabir: The Way of Love and Paradox* Sister Rosemary SLG (1977)
FP62 *Anselm of Canterbury: A Monastic Scholar* Sister Benedicta Ward SLG (1973)
FP63 *Evelyn Underhill, Anglican Mystic: Two Centenary Essays* A. M. Allchin, Bishop Michael Ramsey (1977, 2nd edn 1996)
FP67 *Mary and the Mystery of the Incarnation: An Essay on the Mother of God in the Theology of Karl Barth* Andrew Louth (1977)
FP68 *Trinity and Incarnation in Anglican Tradition* A. M. Allchin (1977)
FP70 *Facing Depression* Gonville ffrench-Beytagh (1978, 2nd edn 2020)
FP71 *The Single Person* Philip Welsh (1979)
FP72 *The Letters of Ammonas, Successor of St Antony* trans. Derwas Chitty, introd. Sebastian Brock (1979, 2nd edn 2023)
FP74 *George Herbert, Priest and Poet* Kenneth Mason (1980)
FP75 *A Study of Wisdom: Three Tracts by the Author of* The Cloud of Unknowing trans. Clifton Wolters (1980)
FP78 *Silence in Prayer and Action* Sister Edmée SLG (1981)
FP81 *The Psalms: Prayer Book of the Bible* Dietrich Bonhoeffer, trans. Sister Isabel SLG (1982)
FP82 *Prayer & Holiness: The Icon of Man Renewed in God* Dumitru Stăniloae (1982, rev. 2023)
FP85 *Walter Hilton: Eight Chapters on Perfection & Angels' Song* trans. Rosemary Dorward (1983)
FP88 *Creative Suffering* Iulia de Beausobre (1989)
FP90 *Bringing Forth Christ: Five Feasts of the Child Jesus by St Bonaventure* trans. Eric Doyle OFM (1984)
FP92 *Gentleness in John of the Cross* Thomas Kane (1985)
FP93 *Prayer: The Work of the Spirit* Sister Edmée SLG (1985)
FP94 *Saint Gregory Nazianzen: Selected Poems* trans. John McGuckin (1986)

FP95 *The World of the Desert Fathers: Stories & Sayings from the Anonymous Series of the Apophthegmata Patrum* trans. Columba Stewart OSB (1986, 2nd edn 2020)

FP104 *Growing Old with God* Timothy N. Rudd (1988, 2nd edn 2020)

FP105 *The Simplicity of Prayer: Extracts from the Teaching of Mother Mary Clare SLG* Mother Mary Clare SLG (1988)

FP106 *Julian Reconsidered* Kenneth Leech, Sister Benedicta Ward SLG (1988)

FP108 *The Unicorn: Meditations on the Love of God* Harry Galbraith Miller (1989)

FP109 *The Creativity of Diminishment* Sister Anke (1990)

FP111 *A Kind of Watershed: An Anglican Lay View of Sacramental Confession* Christine North (1990, 2nd edn 2022)

FP116 *Jesus, the Living Lord* Bishop Michael Ramsey (1992)

FP117 *The Spirituality of Saint Cuthbert* Sister Benedicta Ward SLG (1992)

FP120 *The Monastic Letters of Saint Athanasius the Great* trans. and introd. Leslie Barnard (1994, 2nd edn 2023)

FP122 *The Hidden Joy* Sister Jane SLG, ed. Dorothy Sutherland (1994)

FP124 *Prayer of the Heart: An Approach to Silent Prayer and Prayer in the Night* Alexander Ryrie (1995, 3rd edn 2020)

FP125 *Whole Christ: The Spirituality of Ministry* Philip Seddon (1996)

FP127 *Apostolate and the Mirrors of Paradox* Sydney Evans, ed. Andrew Linzey & Brian Horne (1996)

FP128 *The Wisdom of Saint Isaac the Syrian* Sebastian Brock (1997)

FP129 *Saint Thérèse of Lisieux: Her Relevance for Today* Sister Eileen Mary SLG (1997)

FP130 *Expectations: Five Addresses for Those Beginning Ministry* Sister Edmée SLG (1997)

FP131 *Scenes from Animal Life: Fables for the Enneagram Types* Waltraud Kirschke, trans. Sister Isabel SLG (1998)

FP132 *Praying the Word of God: The Use of* Lectio Divina Charles Dumont OCSO (1999)

FP134 *The Hidden Way of Love: Jean-Pierre de Caussade's Spirituality of Abandonment* Barry Conaway (1999)

FP135 *Shepherd and Servant: The Spiritual Theology of Saint Dunstan* Douglas Dales (2000)

FP136 *Eternity and Time* Dumitru Stăniloae, trans. A. M. Allchin (2001)

FP137 *Pilgrimage of the Heart* Sister Benedicta Ward SLG (2001)

FP138 *Mixed Life* Walter Hilton, trans. Rosemary Dorward (2001)

FP139 *In the Footsteps of the Lord: The Teaching of Abba Isaiah of Scetis* John Chryssavgis & Luke Penkett (2001, 2nd edn 2023)

FP140 *A Great Joy: Reflections on the Meaning of Christmas* Kenneth Mason (2001)

FP141 *Bede and the Psalter* Sister Benedicta Ward SLG (2002)

FP142 *Abhishiktananda: A Memoir of Dom Henri Le Saux* Murray Rogers, David Barton (2003)

FP143 *Friendship in God: The Encounter of Evelyn Underhill & Sorella Maria of Campello* A. M. Allchin (2003)

FP144 *Christian Imagination in Poetry and Polity: Some Anglican Voices from Temple to Herbert* Bishop Rowan Williams (2004)

FP145 *The Reflections of Abba Zosimas: Monk of the Palestinian Desert* trans. and introd. John Chryssavgis (2005, 3rd edn 2022)

FP146 *The Gift of Theology: The Trinitarian Vision of Ann Griffiths and Elizabeth of Dijon* A. M. Allchin (2005)

FP147 *Sacrifice and Spirit* Bishop Michael Ramsey (2005)

FP148 *Saint John Cassian on Prayer* trans. A. M Casiday (2006)

FP149 *Hymns of Saint Ephrem the Syrian* trans. Mary Hansbury (2006)

FP150 *Suffering: Why All this Suffering? What Do I Do about It?* — Reinhard Körner OCD, trans. Sister Avis Mary SLG (2006)

FP151 *A True Easter: The Synod of Whitby 664 AD* — Sister Benedicta Ward SLG (2007)

FP152 *Prayer as Self-Offering* — Alexander Ryrie (2007)

FP153 *From Perfection to the Elixir: How George Herbert Fashioned a Famous Poem* — Benedick de la Mare (2008)

FP154 *The Jesus Prayer: Gospel Soundings* — Sister Pauline Margaret CHN (2008)

FP155 *Loving God Whatever: Through the Year with Sister Jane* — Sister Jane SLG (2006)

FP156 *Prayer and Meditation for a Sleepless Night* — SISTERS OF THE LOVE OF GOD (1993, 2nd edn 2009)

FP157 *Being There: Caring for the Bereaved* — John Porter (2009)

FP158 *Learn to Be at Peace: The Practice of Stillness* — Andrew Norman (2010)

FP159 *From Holy Week to Easter* — George Pattison (2010)

FP160 *Strength in Weakness: The Scandal of the Cross* — John W. Rogerson (2010)

FP161 *Augustine Baker: Frontiers of the Spirit* — Victor de Waal (2010)

FP162 *Out of the Depths* — Gonville ffrench-Beytagh; epilogue Wendy Robinson (1990, 2nd edn 2010)

FP163 *God and Darkness: A Carmelite Perspective* — Gemma Hinricher OCD, trans. Sister Avis Mary SLG (2010)

FP164 *The Gift of Joy* — Curtis Almquist SSJE (2011)

FP165 *'I Have Called You Friends': Suggestions for the Spiritual Life Based on the Farewell Discourses of Jesus* — Reinhard Körner OCD (2012)

FP166 *Leisure* — Mother Mary Clare SLG (2012)

FP167 *Carmelite Ascent: An Introduction to Saint Teresa and Saint John of the Cross* — Mother Mary Clare SLG (rev. 2012)

FP168 *Ann Griffiths and Her Writings* — Llewellyn Cumings (2012)

FP169 *The Our Father* — Sister Benedicta Ward SLG (2012)

FP170 *Exploring Silence* — Wendy Robinson (1974, 3rd edn 2013)

FP171 *The Spiritual Wisdom of the Syriac Book of Steps* — Robert A. Kitchen (2013)

FP172 *The Prayer of Silence* — Alexander Ryrie (2012)

FP173 *On Tour in Byzantium: Excerpts from The Spiritual Meadow of John Moschus* — Ralph Martin SSM (2013)

FP174 *Monastic Life* — Bonnie Thurston (2016)

FP175 *Shall All Be Well? Reflections for Holy Week* — Graham Ward (2015)

FP176 *Solitude and Communion: Papers on the Hermit Life* — ed. A. M. Allchin (2015)

FP177 *The Prayers of Jacob of Serugh* — ed. Mary Hansbury (2015)

FP178 *The Monastic Hours of Prayer* — Sister Benedicta Ward SLG (2016)

FP179 *The Desert of the Heart: Daily Readings with the Desert Fathers* — trans. Sister Benedicta Ward SLG (2016)

FP180 *In Company with Christ: Lent, Palm Sunday, Good Friday & Easter to Pentecost* — Sister Benedicta Ward SLG (2016)

FP181 *Lazarus: Come Out! Reflections on John 11* — Bonnie Thurston (2017)

FP182 *Unknowing & Astonishment: Meditations on Faith for the Long Haul* — Christopher Scott (2018)

FP183 *Pondering, Praying, Preaching: Romans 8* — Bonnie Thurston (2019, 2nd edn 2021)

FP184 *Shem`on the Graceful: Discourse on the Solitary Life* — trans. with introd. Mary Hansbury (2020)

FP185 *God Under My Roof: Celtic Songs and Blessings* — Esther de Waal (2020)

FP186 *Journeying with the Jesus Prayer* James F. Wellington (2020)
FP187 *Poet of the Word: Re-reading Scripture with Ephraem the Syrian* Aelred Partridge OC (2020)
FP188 *Identity and Ritual* Alan Griffiths (2021)
FP189 *River of the Spirit: The Spirituality of Simon Barrington-Ward* Andy Lord (2021)
FP190 *Prayer and the Struggle against Evil* John Barton, Daniel Lloyd, James Ramsay, Alexander Ryrie (2021)
FP191 *Dante's Spiritual Journey: A Reading of the Divine Comedy* Tony Dickinson (2021)
FP192 *Jesus the Undistorted Image of God* John Townroe (2022)
FP193 *Our Deepest Desire: Prayer, Fasting & Almsgiving in the Writings of Saint Augustine of Hippo* Sister Susan SLG (2022)
FP194 *Lent with George Herbert* Tony Dickinson (2022)
FP195 *Four Ways to the Cross* Tony Dickinson (2022)
FP196 *Anselm of Canterbury, Teacher of Prayer* Sister Benedicta Ward SLG (2022)
FP197 *With One Heart and Mind: Prayers out of Stillness* Anthony Kemp (2023)
FP198 *Sayings of the Urban Fathers & Mothers* James Ashdown (2023)
FP199 *Doors* Sister Raphael SLG (2023)
FP200 *Monastic Vocation* SISTERS OF THE LOVE OF GOD, Bishop Rowan Williams (2021)
FP201 *An Ecology of the Heart: Faith Through the Climate Crisis* Duncan Forbes (2023)
FP202 *'In the image of the Image': Gregory of Nyssa's Opposition to Slavery* Adam Couchman (2023)
FP203 *Gregory of Nyssa and the Sins of Asia Minor* Jonathan Farrugia (2023)
FP204 *Discovery* Arthur Bell (2023)
FP205 *Living Healing: the Spirituality of Leanne Payne* Andy Lord (2023)
FP206 *Still Listening: Sowing the Seeds of the Jesus Prayer* Bruce Batstone CJN (2023)
FP207 *Julian of Norwich: Four Essays to Commemorate 650 Years of The Revelations of Divine Love* Sr Elizabeth Ruth Obbard OC, Father Colin SWG, Bishop Graham Usher, Mother Hilary Crupi OJN (2023)
FP208 *Pearls of Life: A Lifebelt for the Spirit* Tony Dickinson (2023)

CONTEMPLATIVE POETRY SERIES

CP1 *Amado Nervo: Poems of Faith and Doubt* trans. John Gallas (2021)
CP2 *Anglo-Saxon Poets: The High Roof of Heaven* trans. John Gallas (2021)
CP3 *Middle English Poets: Where Grace Grows Ever Green* ed. John Gallas (2021)
CP4 *Selected Poems: The Voice inside Our Home* Edward Clarke (2022)
CP5 *Women & God: Drops in the Sea of Time* trans. & ed. John Gallas (2022)
CP6 *Gabrielle de Coignard & Vittoria Colonna: Fly Not Too High* trans. John Gallas (2022)
CP7 *Selected Poems: Chancing on Sanctity* James Ramsay (2022)
CP8 *Gabriela Mistral: This Far Place* trans. John Gallas (2023)
CP9 *Henry Vaughan & George Herbert: Divine Themes and Celestial Praise* ed. Edward Clarke (2023)
CP10 *Love Will Come with Fire* SISTERS OF THE LOVE OF GOD (2023)
CP11 *Touchpapers* collected & trans. John Gallas (2023)

VESTRY GUIDES

VG1 *The Visiting Minister: How to Welcome Visiting Clergy to Your Church* Paul Monk (2021)
VG2 *Help! No Minister! or Please Take the Service* Paul Monk (2022)

slgpress.co.uk